D0775181

MAKING ETHICAL CHOICES
A GUIDE FOR STAFF

MARK A. HENRY

James A. Gondles, Jr., Executive Director
Gabriella M. Daley, Director, Communications and Publications
Leslie A. Maxam, Assistant Director,
    Communications and Publications
Alice Fins, Publications Managing Editor
Michael Kelly, Associate Editor
Sherry Wulfekuhle, Editorial Assistant
Dana M. Murray, Graphics and Production Manager
Stephen Battista, Graphics and Production Associate
Cover by Stephen Battista. Photo courtesy PhotoDisc

Thanks to the *Corrections Today* staff who originally published this
material in June, July, and August of 1998.

Printed in the United States of America by IPI, Upper Marlboro, Maryland.

This publication may be ordered from:
American Correctional Association
4380 Forbes Boulevard
Lanham, Maryland 20706-4322
1-800-222-5646

For information on publications and videos available from ACA,
contact our worldwide web home page at:

http://www.corrections.com/aca

Library of Congress Cataloging-in-Publication Data

Henry, Mark A.
    Making ethical choices : a guide for staff / Mark A. Henry.
        p.   cm.
    ISBN 1-56991-111-8
    1. Correctional personnel--Professional ethics--United States.
    2. Corrections--Moral and ethical aspects--United States.
    3. Prisons--Officials and employees--professional ethics--United States. 4. Prison
    administration--Moral and ethical aspects--United States.   I. Title.
    HV9470.H45   1999
    174'.9365--dc21
                                                                    98-55709
                                                                    CIP

FOREWORD

Most people are ethical and behave appropriately, but some people in positions of responsibility will abuse those positions by engaging in unethical conduct. This occurs in corrections as well. A few employees have carried drugs into institutions, have become sexually involved with offenders, and have participated in the physical abuse of inmates. This conduct compromises the security and integrity of the organization. It presents a danger for staff and offenders alike, and it is a flagrant assault on the mission of corrections.

Unethical behavior is not limited to issues of drugs, sex, and violence, however. No less threatening to corrections are more subtle examples of poor ethical choices by employees such as the use of institutional property for personal use, insubordination, and inattention to duty. Even when not on the job, employees engaging in misconduct can represent a problem for a correctional organization, as there is a connection between the off-duty actions of correctional employees and their ability to do their jobs properly. While the majority of correctional staff perform their duties with honesty and diligence, there always will be a few who yield to the temptations that their jobs present.

In *Making Ethical Choices: A Guide for Staff*, Mark A. Henry discusses the importance of maintaining ethical integrity and delves into the types of unethical behavior most often encountered in corrections: abuse of inmates; inappropriate relationships; introduction of contraband; fiscal improprieties; misconduct while on duty and off; and investigative violations. He uses hypothetical examples to illustrate each of these with a realistic perspective. Henry's book is useful for not only identifying unethical behavior, but responding to it as well. He also offers suggestions to prevent situations from developing into inappropriate conduct.

When correctional employees engage in unethical conduct, they jeopardize their careers, put themselves and others at risk, and tarnish the image of their profession. We believe that this book is an important addition to the tools needed to help corrections professionals make critical, ethical decisions.

James A. Gondles, Jr.
Executive Director
American Correctional Association

Part One

A Guide to Identifying _____
and Investigating Staff Misconduct

A security guard at a large Midwestern manufacturing plant was charged with ensuring that the entrance gate of the plant was secure and that the plant's employees did not steal anything. This individual was very diligent in the performance of his duties and was always on the lookout for would-be thieves. One day, he began to suspect that a certain employee was stealing from the plant. From that day forward, the security guard searched this employee's wheelbarrow every day as he left the plant; however, he never found any stolen property. This went on for twenty years, until the security guard retired.

One day while walking down the street, the retired security guard saw the individual he suspected was stealing from the company. Unable to control his curiosity any longer, he approached the person and said, "I was the security guard at the plant where you worked. Do you remember me?" "Of course," the man replied. The security guard then said, "I know you were stealing from the plant all those years. What were you stealing?" And the man replied, "Wheelbarrows."

Many of those reading this story could have foretold its ending. But the answer was not as obvious to others. So, it is with the topic of ethical behavior by correctional workers. While certain standards of behavior should be implied in any workplace, the unique setting of a prison gives rise to questions about what constitutes ethical and unethical behavior.

Inmates do not stop their manipulative behavior once they reach prison. If anything, it increases as they seek new ways to beat the system. So, it should come as no surprise that correctional staff often are victims of such manipulation. The focus of the ensuing pages is to offer insights and suggestions to correctional managers and supervisors on how to ensure ethical behavior in a sometimes unethical place.

WHAT IS ETHICAL BEHAVIOR?

In order to discuss the importance of ethical behavior by corrections staff, it is first necessary to define what one means by the term, "ethical behavior." According to *Webster's II New Riverside University Dictionary*, ethical behavior is defined as "behavior conforming to accepted principles of right and wrong that govern the conduct of a profession."

The general public has an expectation that when a person convicted of a crime is sentenced to a term of imprisonment, he or she will be confined in a correctional facility that is safe, secure, and operated in a manner consistent with the Constitution of the United States. In addition, the public expects that inmates, once confined, will have very little chance to continue their criminal behavior.

In conjunction with the public's expectations about the behavior of inmates, there is a clear expectation that those employees working in correctional facilities will carry out their assigned duties and responsibilities in ways that provide safe, secure, and humane care to those in their custody.

Unethical behavior by correctional workers does not contribute to this mission. In fact, unethical behavior impacts in a very negative manner on the managers of correctional facilities and their ability to ensure that the mission of their institutions is successfully achieved. Each time the public hears about the unethical behavior of a correctional officer, it diminishes public confidence in the government's ability to protect society.

Another equally important reason for ensuring ethical behavior by correctional workers is that it relates directly to the safety of the staff and inmates who work and reside in correctional facilities. Unethical behavior poses a direct threat to the overall security of a correctional environment in the form of escape plots, inmate assaults, and inmate disturbances.

Unethical behavior by staff undermines the relationship between staff and inmates. Inmates desire the certainty that staff will follow the established rules of the prison. Unethical behavior by staff causes inmates to doubt how the roles of inmates and staff play out inside an institution, and whether staff can be trusted to protect inmates.

Unethical behavior also has an impact on the supervisor/subordinate relationship. Supervisors must trust their subordinate staff to carry out their duties in an ethical manner. When staff act in an unethical way, the faith and trust that supervisors place in them, and indirectly, in all their staff, may diminish.

We live in a time when personal responsibility for one's actions is not expected or fashionable. The terms right and wrong and moral compass do not have the same impact that they did ten or twenty years ago. Instead, we have become accustomed to such expressions as "it's not my fault," or "who knows what's right or wrong anymore?" A generation of employees has entered the workplace without a sense of direction, adrift in a sea of uncertainty as to how to direct or control their behavior both on and off the job.

This moral dilemma exists also in the correctional workplace. Young, inexperienced workers enter correctional facilities ill-prepared by their parents, schools, and society to deal with the ethically challenging environment they will face. However, it is the job of all correctional supervisors to assist their staff in meeting the ethical challenges found in correctional institutions.

TYPES OF UNETHICAL BEHAVIOR

While the kinds of unethical behavior that occur in a correctional setting cover a host of activities, the following are encountered most often:

- Abuse of inmates
- Inappropriate relationships with inmates
- Introduction of contraband
- Fiscal improprieties
- On-duty misconduct
- Off-duty misconduct
- Investigative violations

Abuse of Inmates

The abuse inflicted on the inmate population can take several forms, including physical, emotional, mental, and sexual. Physical abuse of an inmate can range from misapplication of restraint equipment to beating. Verbal, mental, and emotional abuse can include such actions as the use of obscene or degrading language and racial slurs. Forms of nonphysical abuse range from the denial of basic supplies, equipment or services to making inappropriate comments about an inmate's family members.

Inappropriate Relationship with Inmates

Inappropriate relationships with inmates can include bribery; conflicts of interest; solicitation or acceptance of gifts, favors and services from inmates, ex-inmates, relatives, or friends; the offering or giving of gifts, favors, and services to inmates, ex-inmates, relatives, or friends; improper contact or failure to report contact with inmates, ex-inmates, relatives, or friends; and the appearance of inappropriate relationships.

Introduction of Contraband

This type of unethical behavior draws the most public attention. The introduction of contraband—anything not authorized to be brought into a correctional environment, including food, clothing, publications, cosmetics, weapons, escape paraphernalia, money, or drugs—by a staff member in exchange for receiving something of value is the type of behavior most often encountered in this category. It should be noted that most correctional facilities make a differentiation between hard contraband, which are items that could adversely impact the security of the prison, and soft contraband, which is viewed as more of a nuisance than a security threat.

3

Fiscal Improprieties

The behavior found in this area usually involves some type of abuse or misuse of fiscal or business office practices in a correctional environment. Examples include converting institutional property to an employee's personal use, falsification of hours worked, improper procurement practices, and theft or misuse of inmate funds and/or personal property.

On-duty Misconduct

Examples of on-duty misconduct include insubordination; refusal of a direct order; inattention to duty; failure to respond to emergencies; failure to properly supervise inmates; breach of institution security; falsification of records or documents; gambling or the promotion of gambling; loss of temper in the presence of inmates; favoritism on the job; and inappropriate supervisor/subordinate relationships. These types of misconduct usually relate to staff members' failure or refusal to complete their assigned duties as required by their supervisors. Such activities range from inattention to duty (falling asleep on the post) to breach of institution security (losing their keys). The common link here is that the employee's unethical behavior places the security of the institution in jeopardy.

Off-duty Misconduct

This type of unethical behavior takes place off the job; however, the behavior is brought to the attention of the supervisor. The importance of establishing a connection between the misconduct away from work and how it negatively impacts on the employee's ability to do his or her job must be shown. Examples here range from being arrested and convicted of a crime to misuse of an official badge or credential. As with on-duty misconduct, off-duty misconduct by correctional staff has an impact on the public's perception of the profession.

Investigative Violations

Investigative violations occur after the original unethical misconduct takes place. Most attempts to cover up or conceal a material fact or to intimidate witnesses occur during an official investigation. Many times, employees compound their original misconduct by lying about their behavior and trying to get other employees to join in their unethical behavior.

SIGNS OF TROUBLE AHEAD

While it has proven difficult to predict which staff members may engage in unethical behavior, there is some agreement that certain "red flags," or signs of pending trouble, are observable. The following signs of trouble are in no way inclusive, nor do they cover every aspect of staff unethical behavior. However, they do provide clues for the correctional supervisor.

Abuse of Inmates

Supervisors should be observant for a general pattern of complaints. The same staff member or members mentioned by inmates over several allegations should raise a red flag. Supervisors should be cognizant of inmate allegations concerning abuse which contain the same method of abuse with the same circumstances in similar incidents. It is important to note that a staff member receiving allegations of abuse from inmates should look for certain key descriptive phrases describing the abuse, which may be indicative that the allegations have some merit. In addition, supervisors should take care to notice any hardening of an employee's attitude. This usually takes the form of an increased use of slurs and derogatory language toward inmates.

Introduction of Contraband

Again, the supervisor should be aware of a general pattern of complaints against staff, and should be observant of employees who become too familiar or exhibit too close a relationship with a particular inmate or group of inmates. Staff members who spend their off-duty time in the institution or an individual who comes to work very early or stays at the institution very late also should be monitored closely. Those employees who exhibit recent signs of affluence, such as a new car, expensive clothing, or elaborate housing also should be suspect, as these expenditures may be in excess of the individual's take-home pay.

Supervisors also should be cognizant of those employees who are experiencing financial difficulties or marital problems in which the individual has been ordered to pay large amounts of alimony, particularly if this information is well-known to staff and possibly inmates. Employees who express, on a regular basis, negative comments about their feelings of unworthiness or the fact that they are underpaid for the work they are required to perform may be prone to develop inappropriate relationships with inmates. Other areas that should be of concern for supervisors involve inmate mail and telephone use. Regular surveillance of these two sources has provided good information in the past about employees involved in the introduction of contraband.

Fiscal Improprieties

Supervisors should be alert for a consistent pattern of inmate complaints about the lack of supplies, for example, toilet paper, clothing, and certain food items. In addition, supervisors should be particularly aware of an attitude of carelessness among the business office employees in supervising inmates. Often, employees in the business office allow inmates to become too involved in the day-to-day running of the activities in this area, making them susceptible to corruption. Complaints by inmates relating to mismanagement of the commissary should be given special attention by supervisors. In several cases, the inability to provide coveted products has been a prelude to large-scale misconduct by staff. Supervisors should be concerned with monitoring the proper accountability of agency property and supplies within their own area of responsibility.

Supervisors should ensure that time and attendance records are processed according to policy. It is wise to develop techniques which prevent staff from altering these records after their supervisor has signed them. All receiving and discharge procedures should be reviewed by supervisors on a regular basis to ensure that inmate property and funds are handled properly. Along with the commissary, this area is well-known for staff misconduct, related to inmates' funds and property.

Inappropriate Relationships with Inmates

Supervisors especially should be aware of a general pattern of complaints by inmates that some staff members tend to spend too much time with certain inmates or groups of inmates. In addition, other staff members may realize that a coworker is becoming too familiar with a particular inmate. All these are indications that an inappropriate relationship with an inmate may have developed. Close personal observation of the individual would be necessary to determine whether additional investigation is required.

On-duty Misconduct

Supervisors especially should be alert for staff conflicts during social occasions. These conflicts should be resolved quickly and those employees involved should be counseled by their supervisors at the earliest opportunity to uncover the crux of the problem. Supervisors should be aware of staff comments that they feel uncomfortable spying on other staff and that they do not feel comfortable reporting staff misconduct. Supervisors must reinforce the idea to these employees that it is their obligation to report violations of rules, regulations, and laws. These employees must be informed that if they do not report violations that they witness, they could be terminated from their own jobs.

Particular attention should be paid to the physical and mental state of employees. Supervisors should be concerned with changes in behavior, including ill temperament, physical exhaustion, poor physical appearance, poor personal hygiene, an inability by an employee to complete projects in a timely manner that he or she once was able to handle easily, and sloppy work on the job. These employees may be candidates for the Employee Assistance Program; however, it is the responsibility of the supervisor to first note the behavior and make the necessary referrals. It also is important for supervisors to remember that they must maintain a professional distance from their subordinates. Often, supervisors become too personally involved in their employees' lives and, as a result, their effectiveness as supervisors suffers.

Off-duty Misconduct

Supervisors should maintain close contact with other law enforcement agencies so that misconduct by a staff member away from work will be reported quickly. Employees who are involved in off-duty misconduct always must be confronted with their behavior, even if no arrest occurs. These employees should be counseled to ensure they understand that as correctional employees, they must maintain an exemplary pattern of behavior away from work, as well as on the job.

INVESTIGATING UNETHICAL BEHAVIOR

Most correctional agencies have realized the importance of having highly trained personnel handle official investigations. These staff receive specialized training in the investigative process. However, on occasion, and given the unique requirements of correctional management, other supervisory personnel may be called upon to conduct investigations. When this occurs, the following guidelines may be of assistance.

In conducting an investigation, one must first develop a plan of action. The investigator should define the allegations and issues; identify a cast of characters (the complainant, witnesses, subjects); determine who is aware of or has information concerning the incident; and obtain all information available concerning the incident.

For the investigative findings to be conclusive, the investigation must proceed in a logical order. Deductive reasoning, from general to specific, should be used to arrive at a conclusion based on the facts of the case.

The following steps in investigating staff misconduct are not all-inclusive; however, they can be used as a general guideline in conducting a thorough investigation.

The Initial Complaint

The warden or chief executive officer should be advised immediately of allegations of misconduct, as they are required by regulation to investigate complaints thoroughly. Should the information received by officials indicate that criminal violations may have occurred, the warden or chief executive officer is required to immediately refer the matter to the appropriate law enforcement agency. In criminal matters, the local law enforcement authority normally will interview the complainant and take a statement.

Avoid Premature Interviewing of the Subject

Ordinarily, the suspected employee should be the last one to be interviewed during the investigation, and then only after all the evidence has been accumulated, including any observations that best may be made through surveillance or other covert means. Contrary to popular belief, corrupt employees generally do not admit their guilt when they are confronted and questioned about suspected misconduct. Ordinarily, it is only when guilty employees are confronted with solid evidence of their misdeeds that they will make an admission. Therefore, as a general rule, one should not confront a suspected employee at the outset of the investigation.

Confidentiality

Access to information regarding an investigation at an institution should be on a need-to-know basis to avoid informing the subject that an investigation is in progress. Confidentiality also is important since correctional administrators would not wish to embarrass or harm an employee who ultimately may be found innocent of wrongdoing. Therefore, information concerning investigations should be shared only with those employees or officials who have a need for that information. In this regard, documents and reports related to an investigation should be kept in a locked safe.

Confidentiality has a second meaning with regard to a supervisor's ability to keep secret information supplied by the complainant or witnesses. Often, their concern is that the subject of the investigation may become aware that they provided information. Witnesses should understand, however, that their statements may be needed as evidence should charges be lodged against the employee and that the supervisor cannot guarantee confidentiality in that regard. Should administrative charges be brought against an employee, that employee will have the right to access information in the file that was forming the basis for the disciplinary action.

Interviewing Witnesses/Obtaining Documentary Evidence

Witnesses should be interviewed carefully and then affidavits can be taken from each witness with relevant knowledge concerning the matter under investigation. It is most helpful for the affidavit to be written in a narrative form and to describe the events in a chronological sequence. An affidavit is prepared, rather than a memorandum, since a sworn statement has greater evidentiary value. However, in criminal matters, consultation with the office of the prosecuting attorney to determine the proper course of action regarding the taking of sworn testimony is recommended. It is important for the investigator to develop some background information on both the complainant and the witnesses that will assist in measuring their credibility and to understand their motivation in providing information.

Regarding inmate informants, it is important to determine whether they previously have made allegations against law enforcement officials or other individuals and whether the information they provided was credible. In addition, the central files of inmates should be examined to determine whether they have a history of making false statements, exhibit psychological or psychiatric problems that would affect the accuracy of their testimony, or display other characteristics, which would reflect on their reliability. The investigator also should be cognizant of the relationship between the employee providing information and the target of the investigation. These individuals may have ulterior motives for providing information in the investigation.

Occasionally, an investigator may need to interview people in the community. During these interviews, tactful questioning should be directed toward obtaining general background information that will assist in understanding their relationship to the situation under investigation and their general position in the community, including their credibility.

The importance of the investigator collecting official documents as evidence cannot be understated. For example, a copy of the correctional roster for a particular day may establish whether the subject of the investigation was on duty at the time and whether his assignment to a particular post would have provided the opportunity to engage in a certain specified misconduct. When investigators obtain documents from other law enforcement agencies, the agency should understand the purpose for which the document has been obtained and the fact that it will be necessary to disclose the document should the employee be administratively charged with misconduct.

When interviewing inmates and employees, investigators should identify themselves and explain the purpose of the interview, at least in general terms. They should guard against disclosing to the subject of the interview more knowledge about the case than the subject needs to respond intelligently to the questions. In addition, investigators should avoid any implication about the guilt or innocence of the person under investigation. During the interview, investigators should maintain an objective and impartial manner, and their demeanor should communicate sensitivity to the issues of privacy. When interviewing individuals in the community, investigators should display their official identification cards or credentials and advise the subjects that they would like to speak with them concerning an investigation of a department of corrections' employee. Tact and diplomacy are required when interviewing persons in the community.

Surveillance

Often, other investigative techniques, in addition to interviews, prove useful. Surveillance of the subject under investigation frequently is required when the misconduct involves some form of ongoing physical behavior. The surveillance should be planned carefully and provide for observation of the subject and concealment of the investigator. Communication should be provided and tested, and there should be adequate backup in the event that something goes wrong. Under no circumstances should investigators place an inmate in a situation that results in improper physical contact with a suspected employee. In cases involving potentially criminal behavior, the assistance of local law enforcement should be enlisted.

Polygraph

Polygraph testing during investigation of employee misconduct may be employed when other efforts to resolve the allegation have failed and the allegation is sensitive and serious in nature. To ensure the judicious use of such examinations, the chief executive officer should approve, in advance, all authorizations to use polygraph testing.

Consensual Monitoring

The use of consensual monitoring and recording is an effective tool in gathering evidence of employee misconduct. Telephone monitoring and body recorders are used most often in investigations concerning inmates and staff. The consensual monitoring of telephone calls between a suspect and another person is undertaken only after approval from the chief executive officer, for the purpose of recording incriminating statements, which may be made by the suspect employee to the caller. The written permission of one party, generally a cooperating inmate, must be obtained prior to monitoring a call. The cooperating party should be briefed carefully so that any appearance of entrapment will be avoided. In some states, the approval of both parties is required before telephonic conversations may be monitored.

The use of a body recorder to monitor and record conversations between a cooperating party and a suspected employee also can be used. A body recorder is used most frequently in situations involving the introduction of contraband, discussions or agreements about contraband, and discussions concerning sex and improper contacts between inmates and staff. Again, the cooperation of the local law enforcement agency is requested in providing technical assistance, specifically in providing the recording equipment. It should be noted that the approval of a higher level official in the correctional agency may be necessary. Federal law prohibits the nonconsensual monitoring or recording of conversations without a court order, and no correctional employee should become involved in such surveillance.

Photographs

The use of photographs to aid in investigations of staff misconduct can be divided into three major areas. First, photographs should be taken of any physical evidence seized during an investigation of staff misconduct. Second, color photographs should be taken of inmates who allegedly have been physically abused or mistreated by staff members with particular reference to close-up, color photographs of injuries such as bruises, cuts, and marks. It is imperative that such evidence be recorded by photograph. Third, photographs may be taken to document staff members during their actual engagement in misconduct. In connection with surveillance, photographs may document, for example, an employee leaving the home of an inmate's wife, sitting in an automobile with an inmate's relative, or dropping contraband in a container from a prison tower. Local law enforcement agencies generally are equipped with apparatus for night photography, as well as with night scopes, and they usually are willing to assist.

Photo Lineups

Photo lineups have similar value when used properly in staff misconduct investigations. A photo lineup can help in cases where inmates either do not know staff members' names or when they know the names but cannot match them with the correct faces. A series of photographs also is helpful for individuals in the community to identify staff who may be engaging in misconduct. For the results of a photo lineup to be reliable, it should consist of eight-to-twelve photos.

Employee Rights During an Investigation

The principles which govern questioning employees during an investigation are relatively simple. If you wish to question employees whose conduct may have violated criminal law, you must advise them that they have the right to remain silent if the answers to your questions might incriminate them. However, it should be noted that investigations involving criminal matters first should be referred to the local law enforcement agency for consideration and/or advice prior to an internal investigation being initiated by your correctional agency.

Conducting a Subject Interview

An interview with the subject of the investigation ordinarily is conducted toward the conclusion of the investigation. This interview should be conducted in an objective manner, and although questioning of the subject employee should be pursued tenaciously and vigorously, investigators should be tactful, polite, and maintain an unbiased position as gatherers of facts. Investigators should identify themselves to the subjects and inform them of the purpose of the interview by setting forth in broad terms the allegations against them and offering them the opportunity to obtain a representative.

At the beginning of the interview, the investigator should provide the employee with warning about the need to be truthful and forthcoming and advise this person of his or her rights. If the employee is a member of a union, he or she may have a union representative present during the interview. It generally is helpful to set ground rules for the representative's role at the beginning of the interview, as this helps the investigator control the situation.

In an official inquiry, investigators normally must be able to demonstrate the work-related basis for their questions. A general rule is that an employee's alleged misconduct either must involve job performance or adversely impact the efficiency of agency operations. The interview should be structured so that the employee being questioned is put in the position of telling the investigator about various events, rather than responding to questions which may be answered by a simple yes or no. This ensures that the subject will answer questions in a narrative fashion. No attempt should be made to coerce an employee. It is important that the investigator always conduct interviews in a professional manner.

At the conclusion of the interview, an affidavit should be taken from the employee. This sworn affidavit should encompass all topics covered during the interview. Should an employee admit to misconduct during the interview, it is particularly important to record the admissions in writing, and have them signed under oath.

The Investigative Report

The final investigative report should be reviewed thoroughly for completeness and accuracy. The format of the report should be as follows:

11

Making Ethical Choices: A Guide for Staff

Introduction:

This should be a brief paragraph which identifies the subject of the allegation, the alleged misconduct, the name of the institution, the name and title of the investigator, and the dates during which the investigation took place. It also should state how the investigation was conducted, for example, by interviews, surveillance of the subject, or other investigative techniques.

Body of the Report:

The body of the report should consist of a series of paragraphs which describe, chronologically or sequentially, the events which took place, the evidence discovered by the investigator to support or refute the allegations, the information provided by each witness who was interviewed, and any evidence obtained from special techniques. It is important that the body of the report be factual and descriptive.

Summary:

The report should end with a summary paragraph which condenses the information contained in the body of the report so that the reader can grab the essence of the investigation quickly. It is the responsibility of the investigator to conclude, based upon the facts gathered during the investigation, whether the alleged staff misconduct occurred or did not occur.

Part Two

Case Studies Exemplify Challenges
Faced in Correctional Environments

U nethical behavior can occur in many situations and involve many people. The following are case studies involving abuse of inmates, inappropriate relationships with inmates, introduction of contraband, and fiscal improprieties. The comments following each case are offered to stimulate discussion, but they are by no means the only possible solutions or courses of action to take in each situation. Rather, administrators and supervisors should follow their own agencies' codes of conduct and policies, and be guided by their own moral compasses.

ABUSE OF INMATES

Case #1

The characters: Officer Able is a thirty-two-year-old correctional worker assigned to the receiving and discharge area in a correctional facility. He has been with the agency for about six years and is described by coworkers as a loner who does not have many friends at the institution.

Inmate Gold is a female offender who is serving a short period of confinement for theft and passing bad checks. This represents her third period of incarceration.

The situation: Officer Able is responsible for processing inmates in and out of the institution, on furlough and work release. He also is responsible for processing mail that comes into the facility. You are the supervisor for the receiving and discharge area and have received a "snitch note" placed under your office door, stating that Officer Able met inmate Gold at his apartment when she went out on her last furlough. The note makes a vague reference to other favors Officer Able has done for the inmate.

13

Questions for discussion:

1. *What do you do with the note?*
2. *In looking back at the situation, were there any signs of trouble? If so, what were they?*
3. *What do you think should be done with Officer Able if you find that there was unethical behavior?*

Discussion: In taking the note and reporting to your supervisor, you begin the investigative process to determine what happened here. In looking back at this situation, the lack of friendships at work may have offered clues about how Officer Able might interact with the inmate population; perhaps not. The continued employment of this officer would need to be examined closely if an investigation revealed that Officer Able had provided favors for the inmate.

Case #2

The characters: Officer Green is a forty-five-year-old correctional officer with nineteen years of experience in corrections. He is considered a hard officer, with a reputation for not taking any lip from inmates. Officer Blue is a twenty-five-year-old correctional officer. He has been on the job just six months. He is considered a capable officer who has a bright future with the agency.

Inmate Gray is thirty-two years old. He is a manipulative and criminally sophisticated inmate with a long history of assaultive behavior on both inmates and staff. He is physically strong and is known for his combative attitude.

The situation: Officers Green and Blue are working the special housing unit on the day watch. Throughout their tour of duty and for the last several days, inmate Gray has been disruptive. He has been using obscene and threatening language toward Officer Green. It is evident to Officer Blue that there is a longstanding feud between the two.

Finally, Officer Green tells Officer Blue to come with him to the inmate's cell. Officer Green then proceeds to engage in a bitter exchange of words at the cell door with the inmate. During the exchange, the inmate grabs the officer's shirt. The officer is able to break free; however, the inmate scratches the officer's face several times, inflicting superficial but obvious marks. Officer Blue hits his body alarm and with some assistance, the inmate is restrained.

Some time later, Officer Green goes around the corner to the inmate's cell. He tells Officer Blue to watch the unit and he will be back shortly. Although Officer Blue cannot observe the inmate's cell, he hears the sound of punches being thrown and the inmate crying out for help. When Officer Green returns to the office, he says nothing except to remind Officer Blue that he always takes care of business and correctional officers need to stick together.

Case Studies Exemplify Challenges Faced in Correctional Environments

Questions for discussion:

1. *What, if anything, should Officer Blue do?*
2. *You are assigned to investigate the case after the inmate complains he was beaten.*
3. *How would you conduct the investigation?*
4. *What, if anything, would be the proper sanction to impose on the officer if you concluded he did engage in unethical conduct?*

Discussion: Officer Blue finds himself in a classic position in the correctional environment. If he does nothing, he may find himself in the same situation at a later date. However, if he reports the matter to his supervisor, he runs the risk of alienating his fellow correctional officers. In such situations, staff often have a tendency to take sides. Some will support Officer Green and the actions he took; some will want to see justice done; and still others will want nothing to do with the situation. What if Officer Green confesses to beating the inmate, but claims some type of protected class, for instance, he is an alcoholic. On the other hand, what if Officer Blue lies to the investigator? Who is to blame? You can see how complex these cases can become.

Case #3

The characters: Officer Baker is a rookie correctional officer who has served about six months of a one-year probationary term. He is considered somewhat naive and has been counseled about being too close to the inmate orderlies assigned to the housing area in which he is working.

Inmate Tea is a career criminal who has returned to the institution to serve time for a parole violation. He has a quick wit and an equally quick temper.

The situation: Inmate Tea recently has been assigned as an orderly in the housing unit where Officer Baker is working. Over the last few days, the officer and the inmate have been engaged in what began as verbal teasing and quickly escalated into each party verbally abusing the other. Obscene language, as well as descriptions of each person's family, have become part of their daily routine.

Officer Baker has instructed inmate Tea to clean the inmate bathrooms in preparation for an inspection the next day. Inmate Tea refuses to complete the assignment and the verbal discussion between the two quickly escalates into a major argument. After shouting at the inmate, Officer Baker puts his hand on the inmate after he turns away from the officer. This action results in the inmate pushing the officer. The officer hits his body alarm and with responding officers' assistance, the inmate is subdued.

After the majority of staff have departed, Officer Baker is in the process of moving inmate Tea to the Special Housing Unit. As they begin to descend the stairs with the inmate's hands handcuffed behind his back, the inmate falls down the stairs. The inmate claims that he was pushed down the stairs while Officer Baker claims the inmate stumbled and fell.

Questions for discussion:

1. *Was the outcome of this situation difficult to predict? Why or why not?*
2. *Should this situation have been handled differently by Officer Baker's supervisor? How?*
3. *How would you go about resolving which version of the event will be the official version?*

Discussion: Often, situations that start innocently enough wind up costing people their jobs. The unprofessional way in which Officer Baker dealt with the inmate may have been witnessed by other staff and these staff could have counseled the officer over the inappropriateness of his behavior. However, some staff believe it is not their responsibility to do so.

Officer Baker should not have been placed in a situation where he had further contact with the inmate after other staff responded. For a supervisor to allow such a situation to occur invites disastrous results.

This situation will be difficult to resolve conclusively unless there are other witnesses. If not, you will have to rely on two versions of the matter, the officer's and the inmate's, and you will have to try to reach a conclusion based on conflicting versions of the event.

INAPPROPRIATE BEHAVIOR TOWARD INMATES

Case #4

The characters: Officer Brown is a twenty-one-year-old correctional officer who has been employed in corrections for two years. She is considered bright, ambitious, and somewhat sympathetic toward inmates. Her present assignment is a day watch, working in one of the housing units.

Inmate White is twenty-nine years old. He is a career criminal who has three prior convictions for drug offenses, but is serving his first real period of incarceration. He is assigned as a unit orderly and is friendly with staff, going out of his way to do extra work, saying it helps him pass the time.

The situation: Officer Brown has been working this past quarter as the unit officer and inmate White is one of several orderlies assigned to the unit. Officer Brown has begun to rely on inmate White to keep the unit clean and she has received several compliments on the high level of sanitation in the unit.

Inmate White has been discussing his personal situation with Officer Brown. These discussions have included the problems the inmate has been having with his girlfriend, that is, that she has been unfaithful to him. The inmate has been calling Officer Brown by her first name, without her objection. The other day, the inmate brought the officer a sandwich from the dining room since she had missed lunch.

Although she did not eat the sandwich, she failed to report the situation to her supervisor. Today, the inmate left a birthday card on the desk for her. Officer Brown chose to ignore the card and said nothing about it. When she got home that evening, flowers had been delivered to her home without a card.

Questions for discussion:

1. *What should Officer Brown do?*
2. *Has her behavior violated the standards of ethical behavior expected of correctional workers?*
3. *What will happen in the future between the inmate and the officer?*
4. *What could the officer have done differently to prevent this situation?*

Discussion: There remains much debate about how close an officer should get to the inmates under his or her supervision. Some correctional workers insist that inmates not be permitted to call staff by their first names; others would disagree.

One thing is certain, this situation will not end with the delivery of the flowers. Officer Brown has only one choice, to go to her supervisor and explain that she has interacted in an inappropriate way with inmate White. To do anything else would open the door for the inmate to further manipulate the situation to his advantage. Officer Brown forgot that she must maintain a professional distance between herself and inmates; becoming too personal invites disaster.

Case #5

The characters: Mr. Jerico is a forty-seven-year-old correctional worker who is assigned to the inmate commissary. He has been employed with the same correctional agency for the last seventeen years and is considered dedicated, loyal, and hardworking. He is a no-nonsense person who is considered "firm but fair" by all staff and inmates.

Inmate Teal is a sophisticated inmate approximately the same age as Mr. Jerico. He is doing time for armed bank robbery and is viewed as being highly intelligent. He does not associate with many inmates.

The situation: Approximately one month ago, Mr. Jerico's only surviving relative, his sister, died unexpectedly. Mr. Jerico was very close to his sister, yet he took only a short period of time off work in order to take care of her burial and personal affairs. When he returned to work, he did not share his grief with anyone. Instead, he acted as he always had before; he kept his own counsel.

Inmate Teal was reassigned to the commissary detail from another inmate work assignment. One day, Mr. Jerico caught inmate Teal, by himself, crying in a back storage room. He said nothing to the inmate, but the next day, the inmate told Mr. Jerico he had just been informed by the chaplain that his mother had died. Over the next few weeks, Mr. Jerico began to share his sense of loss over his sister's passing with inmate Teal.

One day, the inmate asked Mr. Jerico for advice on how to deal with his mother's personal affairs and how to go about dealing with an insurance problem. From this discussion, Mr. Jerico allowed inmate Teal to place a call to the "insurance agent." One thing led to another, and eventually Mr. Jerico was caught bringing "soft contraband"—food and other comfort items—to inmate Teal.

Questions for discussion:

1. *Your supervisor, the associate warden, calls you into his office and asks how an employee of Mr. Jerico's experience could do such a thing. What do you say?*
2. *What do you think really happened here?*
3. *What do you think is an appropriate action to take against Mr. Jerico? Why?*

Discussion: We, as supervisors, often are asked by our bosses how we could let our employees involve themselves in such misconduct. Although we can offer educated guesses based on our experiences and observations, the true explanation often remains elusive.

In this situation, Mr. Jerico turned to the inmate commissary worker to share his grief. The fact that an inmate manipulator took advantage of the situation should not be unexpected. The only possible outcome of this case would be to terminate Mr. Jerico. Unfortunately, this employee, with seventeen years of dependable and faithful service, forgot where he worked.

Case #6

The situation: You are a counselor at a community corrections center in a large urban area. One day, your brother decides to visit you from out of town. You take him to a restaurant close to where you live and have a nice meal. As you go to the cashier to pay, you hear a voice say, "I hope you enjoyed your meal, Mr. Smith." You look up and see one of the residents of the community corrections center working behind the register. The inmate goes on to explain that his father owns the restaurant and that he helps him out from time to time. The inmate insists that your meal is free, yet you insist you pay. After paying, you walk down the street with quite a bit on your mind.

Questions for discussion:

1. *What should you do?*
2. *If you report this to your supervisor, is he really going to believe that out of all the restaurants in the city, you just happened to choose this one owned by the father of an inmate?*
3. *How do you propose to make your case, or do you?*

Discussion: You really have only two choices: Report the situation to your supervisor or do not report it and hope it goes away. Ideally, you should report the situation, because not to do so places you in greater harm. If you report the situation in a timely and forthright manner, your supervisor will

Case Studies Exemplify Challenges Faced in Correctional Environments

believe you. You do not need to make your case; you merely need to report to your supervisor and you have fulfilled your obligation.

INTRODUCTION OF CONTRABAND

Case #7

The characters: Officer Kale is a two-year veteran at a high-security correctional facility. He is viewed as quiet and sometimes is perceived as not tough enough to work inside a facility of this nature.

Inmate Wood is serving a life sentence without parole for the murder of several family members.

The situation: One day, Officer Kale is entering the institution to start his evening shift when he drops his lunch bag and out falls serious contraband—drugs and a syringe. When confronted with this evidence, Officer Kale makes a startling admission. Inmate Wood is forcing him to introduce contraband under the threat of killing him. After first disbelieving his motivation, the investigator assigned to this case reports that he believes Officer Kale is not the only officer bringing in contraband under threat of physical harm by inmate Wood. In fact, the investigation has revealed several other occurrences where inmate Wood and his gang have physically assaulted or threatened to assault staff if they did not bring contraband into the facility.

Questions for discussion:

1. When you report this infraction to your supervisor, he tells you that nothing like this could happen in his prison and he sends you back to further investigate. What do you do?
2. During the investigation, you hear from a reliable source that this type of behavior has been going on for some time, yet your source will not confirm it with specific details.
3. You are called by a reporter from the local newspaper one night at home and asked about the situation. Where do you go from here?
4. Looking over the facts, you ask yourself, how could this happen? What can be done to prevent it from happening again?

Discussion: When you go to your supervisor to report on your investigation, go prepared. Make certain that you have the facts and that you have followed sound, deductive reasoning in reaching a conclusion. Even though you are the bearer of bad news, it is not your fault that this situation developed.

However, the situation should serve as the catalyst for an honest, reflective discussion by the administration of the facility. Such discussions will help determine what went wrong and how to put safeguards in place to prevent these situations from happening again.

On the matter of the call from the reporter, as an investigator, your responsibility is to investigate the case; the public information officer should handle all press inquiries. Your duty is to refer the call from the reporter to your supervisor, and he or she will handle it.

Case #8

The situation: You are shopping for a car when you stop by a used car lot and see a car you really like. While looking the car over, the owner of the lot asks where you work, where you live, and so on. You are able to get the price down due to some hard bargaining on your part. You congratulate yourself on getting the car you want at a price you wanted to pay.

A few weeks later, you notice the car is smoking and making strange noises. You take it back to the lot and the manager tells you that it will cost $500 to repair. He then tells you that his nephew is an inmate at the prison where you work. He says he will fix your car for free or allow you to "trade up" to a nicer car if you will see that his nephew is "treated right." He does not ask that you do anything wrong, but "that you just keep an eye on the boy and make certain he has what he needs."

Questions for discussion:

1. What do you do?
2. Have you done anything wrong as of yet?
3. Could you have done anything to protect yourself against this?
4. Why not just forget what he said and sue him?

Discussion: You should thank the owner of the car lot for his "kind offer" and then make a hasty retreat. At this point, you have not done anything wrong; however, you must remove yourself quickly from the situation. Report the matter to your supervisor and follow whatever advice you are given. As for getting your money back, you probably should see a good lawyer.

Case #9

The characters: Mr. Delta is a recreational specialist whose hobby is body-building. He prides himself on his physique and spends a great deal of his time with inmates who also are weight lifters. He is a bit conceited about how he looks; however, he is viewed as a capable and dependable worker.

Inmate Lima is tall and slender, definitely not the weight-lifting type. However, he is on Mr. Delta's recreational work detail. In addition, he is recognized by the institution as a confidential informant who has provided credible information about staff misconduct in the past.

The situation: Several recent urine samples have come back with positive results for anabolic steroids. The institution suspects that these inmates have found a way to get steroids from outside the institution. While the investigation is under way, inmate Lima approaches staff and indicates his belief that Mr. Delta is the source of the steroids entering the institution.

Case Studies Exemplify Challenges Faced in Correctional Environments

You are assigned to conduct this investigation and you must recommend a course of action to the associate warden. Your plan is to search Mr. Delta when he arrives for his shift and then confront him with the results of the search. Your plan is approved and Mr. Delta is searched with negative results.

Questions for discussion:

1. *What happened? Do you have the right information or the wrong person?*
2. *What is your next step? The union representing Mr. Delta is demanding an explanation. What do you say?*
3. *Looking back, could you have done anything differently?*

Discussion: Many times, supervisors jump to conclusions too quickly. Perhaps it is the nature of prison work that compels us to act quickly and decisively. In this case, additional investigation up front may have prevented a hasty decision that you now must explain to the staff member as well as the union. We always must strive to determine the facts and then act, not the other way around.

FISCAL IMPROPRIETIES

Case #10

The situation: You are an associate warden. While shopping at the local mall, a vendor, the manager of a stationery store, makes the following statement to you: "The warden must be getting rich from all the kickbacks he gets from people he allows to do business with the prison." When you ask him to explain what he means, he just winks and says, "You know what I'm talking about. Everybody knows about the warden's special fund."

Questions for discussion:

1. *What is your obligation in this matter?*
2. *If you report this situation, to whom do you report it? How do you report it?*
3. *Do you investigate the matter first, before reporting it to someone?*
4. *What happens if you ask the warden about this and he tells you he is aware of it and will handle it?*

Discussion: Your obligation is straightforward; you are to report such matters to your supervisor. However, in this situation, the warden is the suspect party. What do you do? The warden's supervisor is located at headquarters. If you report the matter and there is nothing to it, you run the risk of committing career suicide. Perhaps some further investigation might help; however, you also run the risk of the warden finding out about your investigation and confronting you about it. You face a tough decision; however, you must report the situation to someone.

Case #11

The characters: Officer Red is a thirty-eight-year-old correctional officer with twelve years of experience working in corrections and is being considered for promotion. He is considered firm and fair in his dealings with inmates. He is well-respected by staff and is president of the employees' club.

Officer Yellow is a twenty-nine-year-old correctional officer with five years of experience working in corrections. He recently transferred from a penitentiary, is disliked by inmates, and is considered a loner by staff. He displays a bitter attitude toward the agency and has a special dislike for the current administration.

The situation: Officers Yellow and Red are selected to attend disturbance-control training. They both travel to the staff training center for this one-week training course. While at the center, the officers socialize, eat some meals together, and have a few beers after the class is over.

Upon returning from the training, Officer Red drops by the business office to turn in his travel voucher. While discussing his paperwork with a business office staff member, he glances down at the desk and sees Officer Yellow's travel paperwork. At a glance, Officer Red can see clearly that Officer Yellow has lied on his voucher. He claimed $18 for dinner one night when Officer Red ate with Officer Yellow at McDonald's.

Officer Red said nothing about what he had seen; however, the next day, Officer Yellow comes to his post to talk. Officer Yellow tells Officer Red that he may have fibbed on his paperwork, but he needed the extra money for bills at home. Officer Yellow reminds Officer Red that everyone cheats on his or her travel vouchers and if Officer Red is questioned, he should deny that they ate together. A few days later, Officer Red is called into the associate warden's office and questioned about the matter.

Questions for discussion:

    1. *What should Officer Red do or say?*
    2. *Has either officer engaged in unethical behavior? If so, how?*
    3. *What would you do in this case to decide on a proper penalty?*

Discussion: Officer Red could confront Officer Yellow and tell him he saw his travel voucher and knows that he lied about it. This will then give Officer Yellow time to correct the problem. If he does not do so, then Officer Red should have no qualms about reporting the matter. If Officer Yellow does not admit his error during the investigation, a stronger penalty would be called for, as this reflects on the honesty and integrity of the officer.

Part Three

Good Correctional Managers
Can Help Staff Succeed

ON-DUTY MISCONDUCT

Case #12

The situation: An inmate being escorted to the lieutenant's office broke from the escorting officers to discard a shank he was carrying. While being restrained, the inmate kicked one of the officers in the face, but control was quickly reestablished. While being shaken down before entering the detention area of the institution, and while handcuffed behind his back, the inmate attempted to kick the officer who was pat-searching him. One of the escorting officers slapped the restrained inmate with an open hand on the side of the head. Another staff member objected in the presence of the inmate to the procedures being employed, and his objections resulted in another officer pushing the complaining officer away from the area.

Questions for discussion:

1. *You are assigned to find out what happened. How would you go about it?*
2. *Could things have been handled differently to prevent this from happening?*
3. *Would additional staff training for situations such as this be beneficial?*

Discussion: Conducting an investigation requires interviewing and taking statements from each staff member involved in a given situation. From these statements, a picture of what happened begins to form. Often, there are two conflicting sides to each situation. This is where corroborative evidence helps determine which version of events to believe. In situations such as this, the supervisor must step in and take charge. Had the supervisor taken control of the situation earlier, after the first assault, subsequent events may not have occurred.

Case #13

The situation: Two employees who have worked together in a correctional facility's personnel office for the past three years always have gotten along. Both employees are considered stable and competent workers who get the job done. Although there have been some minor disagreements in the office, nothing major has ever happened until yesterday.

Yesterday, one of the employees went to the coffeepot and found it empty. This employee accused the other employee of purposely drinking the last cup of coffee without making a new pot. A verbal altercation began and quickly escalated into a physical confrontation with the employees striking each other.

Questions for discussion:

1. *What happened here? How would you determine who was responsible?*
2. *Were there any warning signs that may have indicated that a problem was "brewing"?*
3. *How would you go about ensuring that a similar situation does not occur in the future?*

Discussion: The facts of this case are often very familiar to supervisors. Individuals have concerns and problems that they may bring to work. Supervisors must be aware of these concerns and make sure that personal situations do not have an impact on the workplace. As before, the supervisor must step in and defuse these situations or they may explode and call for official action.

OFF-DUTY MISCONDUCT

Case #14

The situation: A laundry plant foreman who works at a medium-security correctional facility has always wanted more out of his law enforcement career. He has made it clear that he eventually wants a badge and a gun. In fact, he applied for a job as a deputy sheriff with a local sheriff's office, but he was not selected due to his poor eyesight.

However, this minor setback has not deterred the employee from pursuing his ambition to work in local law enforcement. He has a cousin who is a sheriff's deputy and, on occasion, his cousin has permitted him to ride along in his patrol car. One evening, when the employee was riding with his cousin, they became involved in a high-speed chase involving a car full of teenagers, ages sixteen to eighteen. This high-speed chase included speeds in excess of 100 miles per hour and finally resulted in the sheriff's deputy firing several shots into the car he was chasing. All of the deputy's actions were in violation of the sheriff's department's operating procedures.

At the hospital, where the occupants of the car were taken due to injuries they sustained when their car ran off the road, the deputy, as well as the laundry plant foreman, were arrested by state police on numerous charges, including attempted murder and reckless endangerment.

Questions for discussion:

1. *After the employee contacts you, his supervisor, how do you propose telling your boss about what happened?*
2. *What do you believe is your agency's policy on such off-duty activities?*
3. *What is the appropriate action to take to resolve this matter?*

Discussion: Supervisors often must take bad news to their bosses. At these times, the boss wants to know what happened. Supervisors must be accountable for their employees and be prepared to explain their employees' behavior both on and off the job.

Off-duty misconduct reflects back to the correctional institution because the public holds correctional workers to a certain standard. A connection does exist between the off-duty unethical activities of correctional workers and their ability to do their jobs. In this case, the poor judgment that this staff member exercised should preclude his continued employment in corrections.

Case #15

The situation: The supervisor of the mechanical services area at a large, high-security correctional facility is driving on a highway. With the employee is his girlfriend and his two small children. He is currently separated from his wife.

While exceeding the speed limit, the employee is pulled over by the police. During the traffic stop, the employee displays his official identification and tells the police officer that he is responding to an institution emergency. He is given a verbal warning by the police officer and allowed to go on his way.

Questions for discussion:

1. *You are the employee's supervisor and the next day you receive a telephone call from the police relating the incident. What do you do with this information?*
2. *How do you go about instructing your staff on the proper use of their official identification?*
3. *What do you believe should happen to this employee?*

Discussion: You report this information to your supervisor who, in turn, instructs you to investigate the incident. In addition, you are asked to develop a method of training staff on the proper use of their official identification. A period of suspension should have the desired effect of ensuring that this employee does not misuse his official identification again.

Case #16

The situation: You are residing in housing on prison grounds provided by the agency for which you work. A couple who lives next door—the husband is your employee—has had a rocky relationship in recent months. Their arguments have been increasing in frequency as well as volume. Today, while relaxing on your day off, one of the couple's children runs over to your house in a panic. The child tells you that his daddy is hurting his mommy. You rush over to the house and find the husband on the floor of the kitchen, bleeding profusely. His wife stands over him with a butcher knife in her hand. You are able to talk her into giving you the knife.

An investigation conducted by local law enforcement results in two conflicting stories. The wife claims that she picked up the butcher knife to defend herself after her husband attempted to cut her with a knife he took from the kitchen sink. The husband relates that he and his wife had an argument and that he struck his wife with his fist. Without warning, she picked up the butcher knife from the kitchen sink and stabbed him several times.

Questions for discussion:

1. *The police are seeking your guidance in resolving this matter. How do you propose to resolve the case?*
2. *What safeguards should be in place to prevent similar situations from occurring?*
3. *What is your final decision in this case? Whom do you believe? What does the evidence suggest?*

Discussion: As before, you have two conflicting statements about what occurred. And as before, as an investigator in this situation, you must seek to uncover any and all evidence that will lead you to a logical conclusion. In this situation, the child provided key evidence of who was the aggressor, which resulted in the arrest and prosecution of the employee for spousal abuse.

INVESTIGATIVE VIOLATIONS

Case #17

The situation: A new correctional employee and his wife go to a social occasion at another employee's house. During the party, several of the employees and their spouses pass a marijuana cigarette around the den. When he sees this activity, the employee and his wife abruptly leave. On the drive home, his wife inquires about the sudden departure and the employee tells her why. Her question (to her husband) is: "What are you going to do?"

Questions for discussion:

1. *What emotions are present as the employee decides what to do?*
2. *What is his obligation as a correctional employee?*
3. *What might happen if he does nothing?*

Discussion: Many emotions are involved in the decision of "the right thing to do." The staff member wants to fit in with his coworkers and be well liked. However, he also realizes that his employer expects him to report any violations of the employee code of conduct. But the employee's wife does not want her husband to jeopardize his career.

If he chooses to do nothing, other events may occur that will bring the employee's inaction to light. What choices does the employee have and what can his supervisor do to assist him in doing what is right?

Case #18

The situation: During a forced-cell move of a disruptive inmate, the inmate's leg is broken. All of the staff involved write memorandums about what happened. In reviewing these memorandums and other documentation, it is apparent to you, the investigator, that something is not right.

During a follow-up investigation, you find evidence that the supervisor who was involved in the situation is talking to the other staff involved and encouraging them to "do the right thing." When you take your investigative results to this supervisor's boss, he tells you that the supervisor is just trying to ensure a quick resolution. Further, the supervisor's boss tells you not to worry about this matter, as the supervisor is scheduled to be promoted and moved across the state to another prison.

Questions for discussion:

1. *How do you proceed with your investigation?*
2. *Should you take the advice given and drop the matter?*
3. *What do you think will happen to the supervisor in his next job assignment?*

Discussion: This situation puts you, the investigator, in a dangerous situation. If you go higher up the chain of command, you run the risk of adversely affecting your career. If you do nothing and your inaction becomes known, you run the risk of being derelict in your duties. What should you do?

Case #19

The situation: You are assigned to investigate a case that involves allegations of physical abuse of an inmate after a violent confrontation. During your investigation, several of the staff involved in the incident have given you statements that conflict with the physical evidence you have gathered. In other words, you know that someone is lying. The challenge facing you is to determine whether to close your investigation at this point or to give these staff members a second chance to tell the truth.

Questions for discussion:

1. *What is your position on continuing this investigation or closing it unresolved?*
2. *What motivations do staff have to lie to you during an investigation?*
3. *What is "the right thing to do" here?*

Discussion: People do not always tell the complete truth for many reasons. In this case, some staff may think that "doing the right thing" is telling a version of the truth advantageous to their fellow employees. Some will not tell the truth anyway, because the truth will result in disciplinary action against them. A second opportunity will provide those staff attempting to "do the right thing" to tell the complete truth.

HELPING EMPLOYEES SUCCEED

The majority of people who work in correctional facilities throughout this country carry out their assigned duties on a daily basis in the highest ethical manner. However, there are individuals employed in prisons who are not so ethical.

Correctional supervisors and managers can help their staff succeed in their duties and act in an ethical manner. The following ten suggestions may provide guidance to supervisors and staff in their day-to-day dealings with inmates. Although these suggestions do not cover every aspect of correctional work, they provide a good "umbrella" to cover staff as they do their jobs.

1. Make Sure Your Employees Know Policy. It is amazing how many correctional managers and supervisors make the assumption that their staff, particularly those staff who are on the front line supervising inmates, know the policies and procedures of the facility where they work. Never assume that staff know what they are expected to do. Managers need to ask their employees questions and determine firsthand if their employees know the established procedures of an institution. Another vital tool for managers to ensure that their employees know policy is to observe them as they walk around the facility on a daily basis.

No one needs to remind us that inmates know correctional policies and procedures better than we do. If managers do not take the time to teach staff the right way to carry out their duties, inmates inevitably will take the opportunity to do so.

2. Anything Not Inspected Is Neglected. This old prison saying is extremely relevant in pointing out that managers need to get out of their offices and inspect all areas of the prison. Staff are quick to notice when managers do not visit their work areas and as a result, they tend to neglect those parts of their jobs about which they feel management does not care.

Inmates are equally observant and watch closely to see how much attention is paid to various procedures. It is vital that managers make certain that they are equally as interested in and available to their employees as the inmates are.

3. Lead by Example. Managers who lead by example get their messages across loud and clear. Staff and inmates closely watch to determine for themselves if management's words are matched by deeds and/or examples.

If you talk about how vital and necessary ethical behavior is, but your actions send the message that you are willing to cut corners on some rules that you consider unimportant, staff will watch your example and follow in your footsteps. Nothing demoralizes staff more than managers who talk about how ethical behavior is the standard and then turn around and "lower the standard bar" for themselves or others.

This leadership-by-example also is important when managers become aware of unethical behavior. The standard that managers set cannot waver in its application to each employee. How you, as a manager, deal with unethical behavior sends a loud message to the majority of your staff who are conscientiously doing their jobs in an ethical manner.

4. Management Sets a Moral Tone. This concept goes hand-in-hand with the previous suggestion of leading by example. The moral tone or character of a correctional facility is comprised of many parts. However, the most important part is how management defines ethical behavior, what expectations for right and wrong behavior it sets, and guidelines that are offered to staff.

5. Know Your Inmate Manipulators. Make certain that staff at all levels in your facility are aware of manipulative inmates. Their prison records usually are replete with many instances of prior attempts, successful and unsuccessful, to manipulate staff.

There are several proven and effective ways to disseminate this information: posted picture files, intelligence briefings, and staff recalls are a few that come to mind. Whatever method is chosen should be evaluated occasionally to ensure that staff get the message: These manipulative inmates require closer than usual observation. Beware!

6. Be Sure to Document. Another old prison saying is that if an inmate does something that a staff member observes and the staff member does not say "no" to the inmate, he or she has, in fact, said "yes." Staff who become involved in attempts by inmates to involve them in unethical behavior usually are first tested by the inmate. This test typically involves a minor rule infraction to determine if a staff member will say "no" or ignore the behavior. Unless staff say "no" and document the incident by writing a misconduct report or somehow document the attempt by other means, the path toward future unethical behavior becomes a very slippery slope indeed.

7. Take Time to Criticize and Time to Praise. Supervisors must criticize staff's work performance from time to time. However, this criticism should be done in private, if possible, and in a way that maintains staff members' dignity. The other side of the coin is to praise staff when their behavior warrants it. This praise should be delivered in as energetic a manner as possible and with the same degree of attention that criticism is given. Staff closely watch to see if their supervisors take the time to tell them they care. Either criticism or praise is evidence to staff that their supervisors care about them.

8. Look With a "Third Eye." When supervisors walk around institutions, they not only should rely on their five senses, but also on their correctional "third eye," or gut reaction—the hairs on the backs of their necks stand up, or something tells them that the pulse of the institution is just not right. When supervisors walk through institutions, they observe many things. Of these observations, many must be filtered by supervisors' experience and training to determine when they warrant further action.

9. Coaching and Mentoring Are Effective Training Tools. As a supervisor, the majority of conversations with your staff will involve giving constructive criticism and the occasional word of praise. These occasions are not enough to ensure ethical behavior by your staff. Coaching and mentoring require supervisors to work with employees to help them see the reason for the right and wrong nature of ethical behavior. As coaches develop the talents of their teams, so must a supervisor. Likewise, supervisors must be mentors to their staff and bring them along in the right way.

Remember, inmates are standing by to provide this needed guidance and support for those staff yearning for this attention. If they are unable to get this type of important training from you, some will not hesitate to seek it elsewhere.

10. Do Not Become Complacent. Staff and supervisors often want the same thing: a quiet, uneventful shift that ends with them going home in a safe manner. When things are going well, there is a tendency to become complacent. Inmates often contribute to this desire to have things go smoothly. They, too, do not want to "make waves." Supervisors have an obligation to check and monitor their institution's operations continuously to ensure nothing is taken for granted. Things may look all right, but are they?

CONCLUSION

In closing, this warden would like to offer one more piece of advice to those individuals who daily accomplish the dangerous and difficult mission of confining inmates. The story is told of a young man who went to see the president of the company he worked for to find out the secret of his success. When asked the question by the young man, the president replied, "right decisions."

The young man pressed on and asked, "How do you make right decisions?" The president answered, "experience."

"And how do you get experience?" the young man further asked.

To this the president replied, "wrong decisions."

From this author's experience, he knows that the right decisions he has made and the success that has resulted from those decisions have been the results of many wrong decisions. He tips his hat to those brave souls, correctional supervisors, still willing to gain experience by making right, and sometimes wrong, decisions.

REFERENCES

Allen, Bud and Diana Bosta. 1993. *Games Criminals Play*, Sixteenth Edition. Sacramento, California: Rae John Publishers. Available from the American Correctional Association, Lanham, Maryland.

Allen, Harry E. and Clifford E. Simonsen. 1992. *Corrections in America: An Introduction, Sixth Edition.* New York: Macmillan Publishing Co.

American Correctional Association. 1992. *Working with Manipulative Inmates.* Laurel, Maryland: American Correctional Association.

———. 1998. *Ethics in Corrections Video and Leader's Guide.* Lanham, Maryland: American Correctional Association.

Fournies, Ferdinand. 1988. *Why Employees Don't Do What They're Supposed to Do and What to Do About It.* Blue Ridge Summit, Pennsylvania: TAB Books Inc.

Hutton, Scott D. 1998. *Staff Supervision Made Easy.* Lanham, Maryland: American Correctional Association

Kauffman, Kelsey. 1988. *Prison Officers and Their World.* Cambridge, Massachusetts: Harvard University Press.

Runyon, Tom. 1953. *In for Life: A Convict's Story.* New York: W. W. Norton and Co. Inc.

Shostrum, Everett. 1968. *Man the Manipulator.* Nashville, Tennessee: Abingdon Press.

Steiner, Claude. 1974. *Scripts People Live.* New York: Grove Press Inc.

Torok, Lou. 1973. *The Strange World of Prison.* New York: The Bobbs-Merrill Co. Inc.

About the Author

Mark A. Henry started his corrections career in December 1974 as a correctional officer at the U.S. Penitentiary, Lewisburg, Pennsylvania. He has held a number of positions of increasing responsibility at eleven Federal Bureau of Prisons' institutions. He has worked in both the Central and Regional Offices for the Federal Bureau of Prisons, and he has worked in each geographical region, with the exception of the South Central Region.

He first was appointed a warden in 1988. He has held the position of warden at four institutions: Federal Prison Camp, Pensacola, Florida; Metropolitan Correctional Center, Chicago, Illinois; Federal Correctional Institution, Terminal Island, California; and currently he is at the Federal Correctional Institution, Cumberland, Maryland. He holds a Master's degree in criminal justice from John Jay College of Criminal Justice and a Master's degree in public administration from the University of Southern California. Warden Henry is a native of Washington, DC.

Currently, he resides in LaVale, Maryland with his wife and two children.